PIANO • VOCAL • GUITAR

CONTENTS

3	THE BEAUTIFUL BRINY SEA	*Bedknobs and Broomsticks*
6	BEYOND THE SEA	*Finding Nemo*
10	CANDLE ON THE WATER	*Pete's Dragon*
13	DOWN TO THE SEA	*The Little Mermaid II: Return to the Sea*
24	THE ELEGANT CAPTAIN HOOK	*Peter Pan*
32	FATHOMS BELOW	*The Little Mermaid*
27	FINALE (Here on the Land and Sea)	*The Little Mermaid II: Return to the Sea*
38	HAWAIIAN ROLLER COASTER RIDE	*Lilo & Stitch*
44	JUST AROUND THE RIVERBEND	*Pocahontas*
50	LOVE CAME FOR ME	*Splash*
54	A PIRATE'S LIFE	*Peter Pan*
56	UNDER THE SEA	*The Little Mermaid*
70	THE WALRUS AND THE CARPENTER	*Alice in Wonderland*
66	A WHALE OF A TALE	*20,000 Leagues Under the Sea*
68	YO HO (A Pirate's Life for Me)	*Disneyland Park and Magic Kingdom Park*

Disney characters and artwork © Disney Enterpriese, Inc.

ISBN 0-634-07978-6

Walt Disney Music Company
Wonderland Music Company, Inc.

DISTRIBUTED BY

HAL•LEONARD®
CORPORATION

7777 W. BLUEMOUND RD. P.O. BOX 13819 MILWAUKEE, WI 53213

Visit Hal Leonard Online at
www.halleonard.com

THE BEAUTIFUL BRINY SEA

from Walt Disney's BEDKNOBS AND BROOMSTICKS

Words and Music by RICHARD M. SHERMAN
and ROBERT B. SHERMAN

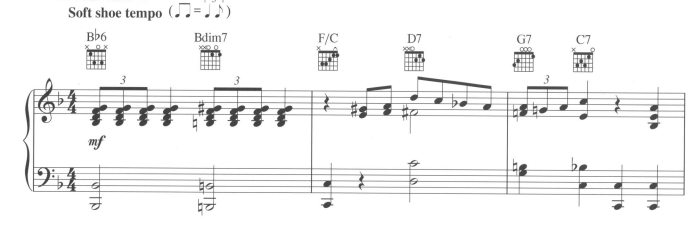

How pleas-ant bob-bing a-long, bob-bing a-long on the bot-tom of the

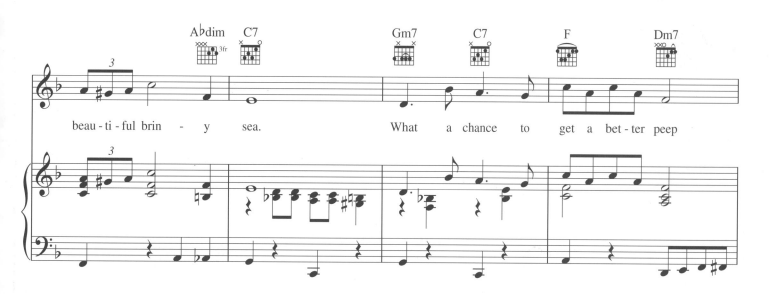

beau-ti-ful brin-y sea. What a chance to get a bet-ter peep

BEYOND THE SEA

Words and Music by CHARLES TRENET,
ALBERT LASRY and JACK LAWRENCE

CANDLE ON THE WATER

from Walt Disney's PETE'S DRAGON

Words and Music by AL KASHA
and JOEL HIRSCHHORN

I'll be your can-dle on the wa-ter, my love for you will al-ways
I'll be your can-dle on the wa-ter 'til ev-'ry wave is warm and

burn. I know you're lost and drift-ing, but the clouds are lift-ing.
bright. My soul is there be-side you, let this can-dle guide you;

Don't give up; you have some-where to turn.
soon you'll see a gold-en stream of light.

DOWN TO THE SEA

from Walt Disney's THE LITTLE MERMAID II: RETURN TO THE SEA

Words and Music by
MICHAEL and PATTY SILVERSHER

Sea Chorus: La la la la dee da da la da dee da dee da da

la la da dee da _____ da

la la ___ dee da da la la ___ dee da la ___

___ la ___ la la dee da. ___ Up from the

THE ELEGANT CAPTAIN HOOK

from Walt Disney's PETER PAN

Words by SAMMY CAHN
Music by SAMMY FAIN

FINALE
(Here on the Land and Sea)
from Walt Disney's THE LITTLE MERMAID II: RETURN TO THE SEA

Words and Music by
MICHAEL and PATTY SILVERSHER

FATHOMS BELOW

from Walt Disney's THE LITTLE MERMAID

Lyrics by HOWARD ASHMAN
Music by ALAN MENKEN

Brightly

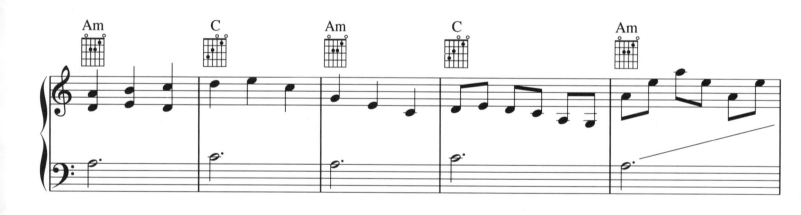

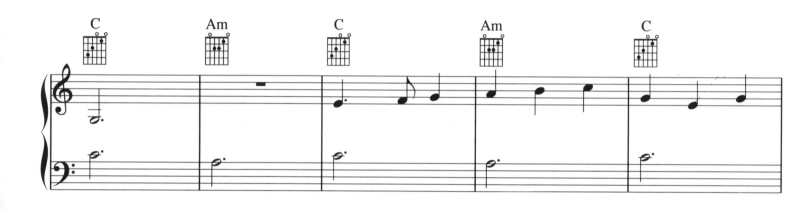

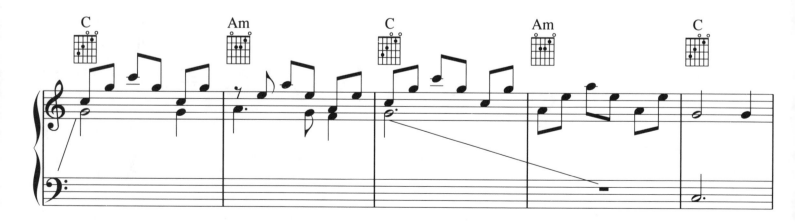

Heave,   ho.

HAWAIIAN ROLLER COASTER RIDE

from Walt Disney's LILO & STITCH

Words and Music by ALAN SILVESTRI
and MARK KEALI'I HO'OMALU

A - lo - ha e, a - lo - ha e, an - o'ai___ ke a - lo - ha
(A - lo - ha e, a - lo - ha e,)

e. A - lo - ha e, a - lo - ha e,
(an - o'ai___ ke a - lo - ha e.) ___ (A - lo - ha e, a - lo - ha

'an o'ai___ ke a - lo ha e.
e,) ('an - o'ai___ ke a - lo - ha e. ___

1., 3. *Lead:* There's no ___ place I'd rath - er be ___ **Chorus:* than on my surf - board out at sea.
2. *All:* There's no ___ place I'd rath - er be ___ *Chorus:* than on the sea - shore dry, wet, free.

*Children's Chorus

Lead: lin - ger - ing ___ in the o - cean blue. ___ *Chorus:* And if I had one wish come true *Lead:* I'd
All: On gold - en sand is ___ where I'd ___ lay, *Chorus:* and if I on - ly had my way *All:* I'd

JUST AROUND THE RIVERBEND

from Walt Disney's POCAHONTAS

Music by ALAN MENKEN
Lyrics by STEPHEN SCHWARTZ

LOVE CAME FOR ME

Love Theme from SPLASH

Music by LEE HOLDRIDGE
Lyrics by WILL JENNINGS

Slowly

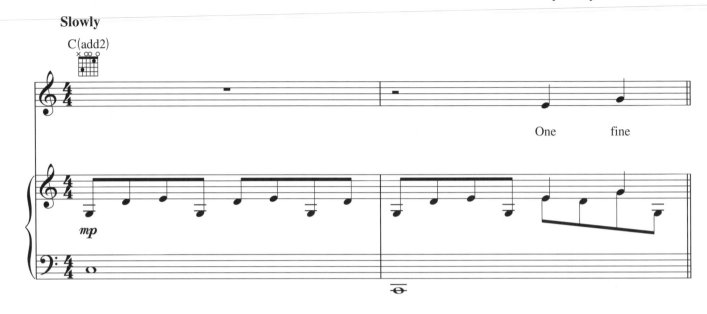

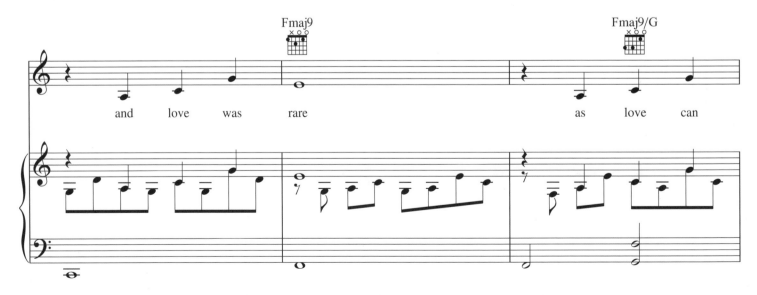

A PIRATE'S LIFE

from Walt Disney's PETER PAN

Words by ED PENNER
Music by OLIVER WALLACE

Moderately, with a bounce

Oh, a pi-rate's life is a won-der-ful life, a-rov-ing o-ver the
Oh, a pi-rate's life is a won-der-ful life with-out a care to be-

sea. Give me a ca-reer as Buc-a-neer, it's the life of a pi-rate for
hold. You car-ry a gun and a jug of rum and your pock-ets are load-ed with

me! Oh! The life of a pi-rate for me!
gold! Oh! Your pock-ets are load-ed with

gold!

UNDER THE SEA

from Walt Disney's THE LITTLE MERMAID

Lyrics by HOWARD ASHMAN
Music by ALAN MENKEN

A WHALE OF A TALE

from Walt Disney's 20,000 LEAGUES UNDER THE SEA

Words and Music by NORMAN GIMBEL
and AL HOFFMAN

YO HO
(A Pirate's Life for Me)
from PIRATES OF THE CARIBBEAN at Disneyland Park and Magic Kingdom Park

Words by XAVIER ATENCIO
Music by GEORGE BRUNS

THE WALRUS AND THE CARPENTER
from Walt Disney's ALICE IN WONDERLAND

Words by BOB HILLIARD
Music by SAMMY FAIN

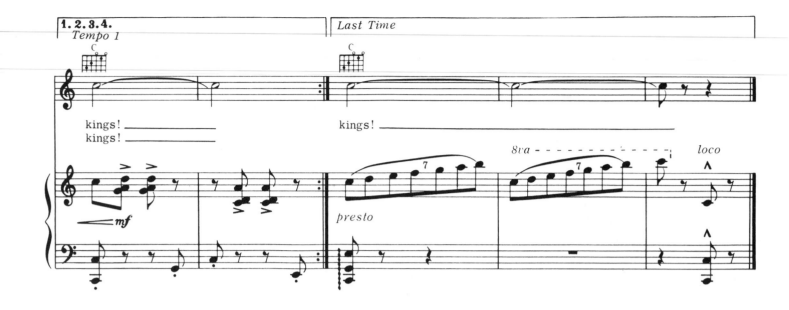

VERSE 3

    So the oysters went to follow and their shells and shoes were neat,
    But I fear my dear you'll find this queer, because they had no feet.
    Soon the oysters all were out of breath, and they said, let's stop and chat,
    'Cause most of us are ready to rest, you see, we're much too fat. (Fat..)

CHORUS

    The time has come, the Walrus said, to speak of other things,
    Of shoes and ships and sealing wax, of cabbages and kings,
    And why the sea is boiling hot, and whether pigs have wings,
    Callooh, callay, we eat today, like cabbages and kings.

VERSE 4

    Said the walrus, just a loaf of bread is exactly what we need,
    And some pepper and some vinegar and very good indeed.
    If you're ready little oyster friends, we can now begin the food,
    But not on us, the oysters all cried as they begun to plead. (Feed. . .)

CHORUS

    The time has come, the oysters cried, to speak of other things,
    Of shoes and ships and sealing wax, of cabbages and kings.
    And why the sea is boiling hot and whether pigs have wings.
    Callooh, callay, we're fools to play with cabbages and kings.

VERSE 5

    Oh, I weep for you, said the Walrus, and I deeply sympathize,
    Then he held his pocket handkerchief before his streaming eyes.
    Little oysters, said the Carpenter, but answer there came none,
    And this was scarcely odd because, they'd eaten every one.. (Oh . .)

CHORUS (Gradually faster and faster)
    The time has come, the Walrus said, to speak of other things,
    Of shoes and ships and sealing wax, of cabbages and kings.
    And why the sea is boiling hot and whether pigs have wings,
    Callooh, callay, a lucky day, for cabbages and kings.